Super Bowl Champions: Chicago Bears

Running back Gale Sayers

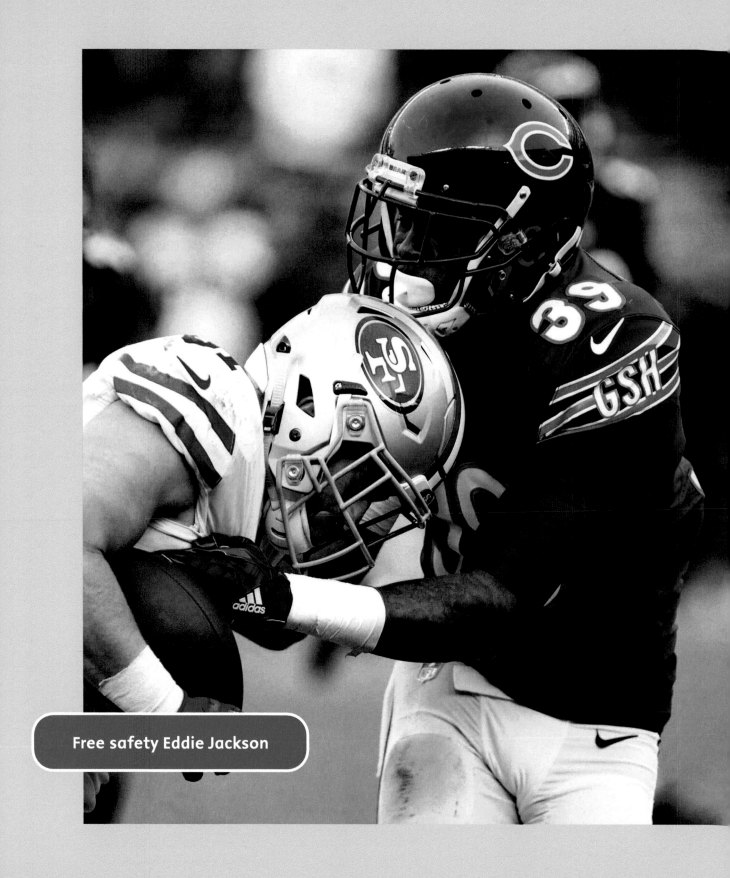

Free safety Eddie Jackson

SUPER BOWL CHAMPIONS

CHICAGO BEARS

MICHAEL E. GOODMAN

CREATIVE EDUCATION / CREATIVE PAPERBACKS

Published by Creative Education and Creative Paperbacks
P.O. Box 227, Mankato, Minnesota 56002
Creative Education and Creative Paperbacks are imprints of
The Creative Company
www.thecreativecompany.us

Design and production by Blue Design (www.bluedes.com)
Art direction by Rita Marshall

Photographs by Alamy (Cal Sport Media), Getty Images
(Bettmann, Corbis, Jonathan Daniel, Bill Eppridge/Time
Life Pictures, Icon Sportswire, Kidwiler Collection/Diamond
Images, Don Lansu, Al Messerschmidt, Pro Football Hall of
Fame, Rob Tringali/SportsChrome), Unsplash.com (Pedro
Lastra)

Library of Congress Cataloging-in-Publication Data
Names: Goodman, Michael E., author.
Title: Chicago Bears / by Michael E. Goodman.
Description: Mankato, Minnesota: Creative Education/
    Creative Paperbacks, 2023. | Series: Creative sports. Super
    Bowl champions | Includes bibliographical references
    and index. | Audience: Ages 6–10 | Audience: Grades
    2–3 | Summary: "Approachable text and engaging photos
    highlight the Chicago Bears' Super Bowl wins and losses,
    plus sensational players associated with the team such as
    Khalil Mack"—Provided by publisher.
Identifiers: LCCN 2021044456 (print) | ISBN 9781640263888
    (library binding) | ISBN 9781628329216 (paperback) | ISBN
    9781640005525 (ebook)
Subjects: LCSH: Chicago Bears (Football team)—Juvenile
    literature.
Classification: LCC GV956.C5 G57 2023 (print) | LCC GV956.C5
    (ebook) | DDC 796.332/640977311—dc23
LC record available at https://lccn.loc.gov/2021044456

Running back Thomas Jones

C O N T E N T S

Home of the Bears

Chicago, Illinois [*il-uh-NOY*], is a busy city in the Midwest. It is famous for Navy **Pier** on Lake Michigan. Chicago is the home of a football team called the Bears. The Bears play at Soldier Field.

The Bears were among the first teams in the National Football League (NFL). One of their main **rivals** is the Green Bay Packers. All NFL teams try to win the Super Bowl. The winner is the champion of the league!

Running back Matt Forte

Naming the Bears

The team's first home in Chicago was Wrigley Field. Baseball's Chicago Cubs already played there. Owner George Halas decided to call the football team the Bears. He said that bears were bigger and meaner than cubs.

Running back Red Grange

Bears History

The Bears team is more than 100 years old. It started playing in 1921. George Halas was the team's first owner and coach. He was called "Papa Bear." He led the Bears to the NFL championship three times in the 1920s and 1930s.

Running backs Red Grange and Bronko Nagurski [*nuh-GER-skee*] were early stars for the Bears. Grange was quick and hard to tackle. Nagurski was powerful. He plowed over the **defense**.

Quarterback Sid Luckman led Chicago to four more **titles** in the 1940s. The 1940 championship game was amazing. The Bears crushed the Washington team, 73–0! That is the most points scored by one team in an NFL game.

Chicago won another NFL championship in 1963. After that, the Bears lost a lot of games. Still, they had some great players. Gale Sayers and Walter Payton were speedy running backs.

Quarterback Sid Luckman

Linebacker Brian Urlacher

In 1985, the Bears could not be stopped. They had a 15–1 record. Then they won Super Bowl XX (20). They beat the New England Patriots, 46–10. The players recorded a song called "The Super Bowl Shuffle." It was a big hit!

The Bears were strong in 2006. The team's leader was linebacker Brian Urlacher [*ER-lak-er*]. He made many tackles. Chicago reached the Super Bowl that season. Devin Hester returned the opening kickoff for a **touchdown**. But the Bears lost to the Indianapolis Colts.

Other Bears Stars

The Bears have had many powerful linebackers. In the 1960s, runners feared being tackled by Dick Butkus. He once said, "I was **fierce** . . . I was tough." Linebacker Mike Singletary played on the 1985 championship team. He played like he was angry at the other team.

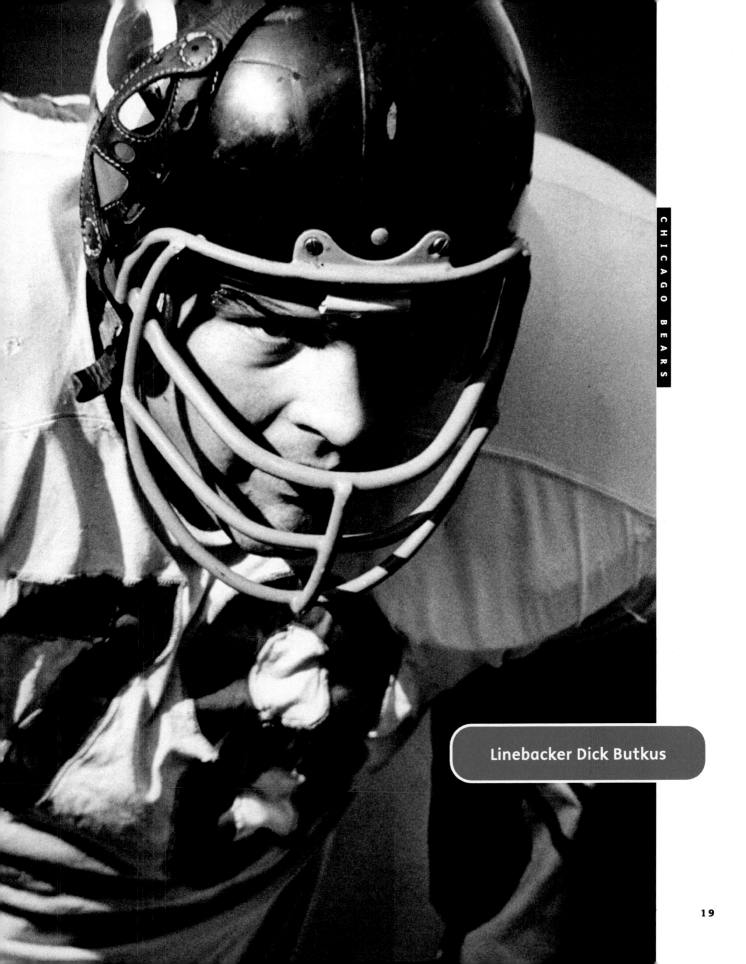

Linebacker Dick Butkus

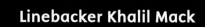
Linebacker Khalil Mack

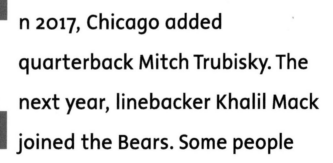

In 2017, Chicago added quarterback Mitch Trubisky. The next year, linebacker Khalil Mack joined the Bears. Some people think he is the best defensive player in the NFL. Bears fans hope these stars will soon lead Chicago to another championship.

About the Bears

Started playing: 1921

. . . .

Conference/division: National Football
Conference, North Division

. . . .

Team colors: dark navy blue and orange

. . . .

Home stadium: Soldier Field

. . . .

SUPER BOWL VICTORY:

XX, January 26, 1986, 46–10 over New
England Patriots

. . . .

Chicago Bears website:
www.chicagobears.com

. . . .

Glossary

defense — the players who try to keep the other team from scoring

....

fierce — mean or violent

....

offense — the players who control the ball and try to score

....

pier — a landing place for boats and ships

....

rivals — teams that play extra hard against each other

....

titles — in sports, another word for championships

....

touchdown — a play in which a player carries the ball into or catches the ball in the other team's end zone to score six points

....

Wide receiver Allen Robinson

Index